Let's Race

By Donna Latham

Illustrated by Priscilla Burris

Target Skill Realism and Fantasy

We are running.

We run in the sun!

We are skipping.

We skip and run.

My mom and dad run.

My sis is running too.

I like to skip and run.

I like to jump in the leaves!

It is time to go home.

We go into our den.

It is getting dark and cold outside.

Mom and Dad tuck us in bed.

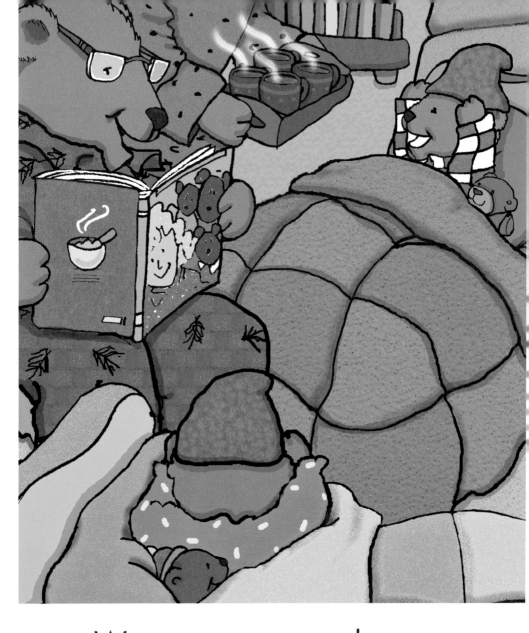

We put on our red caps.
We get set for a long,
long nap!